ROMANTIC TRAPEZOID

Victor L Cahn

BROADWAY PLAY PUBLISHING INC
New York
www.broadwayplaypub.com
info@broadwayplaypub.com

ROMANTIC TRAPEZOID
© Copyright 2019 Victor L Cahn

Cover art by Billy Mitchell

First edition: January 2019
I S B N: 978-0-88145-809-1

Book design: Marie Donovan
Page make-up: Adobe InDesign
Typeface: Palatino

The world premiere of ROMANTIC TRAPEZOID was produced by Rachel Reiner Productions, LLC at the Lion Theatre @ Theatre Row in New York on 8 November 2017. The cast and creative contributors were:

DAVE..Zach Calhoon
MELISSA.................................Elizabeth Inghram
BETH.. Joy Donze

Director......................................Alberto Bonilla
Set designer....................................... Sheryl Liu
Costume designer....................Viviane Galloway
Lighting designer.........................Pamela Kupper
Sound designer..................................Nick Simone
Stage manager........................... Jasmin Sanchez
Production manager ....Jenna R Lazar

CHARACTERS & SETTING

DAVE, 35+, *intellectual, dryly witty*
MELISSA, 30+, *spirited, alluring*
BETH, 26+, *smaller than* MELISSA, *sexy and effusive*

The Place: MELISSA's *one-bedroom apartment in Manhattan.*

At center are a sofa and a coffee table. To either side are a closet, a chest of drawers, a desk and chair, and the kitchen and dining area. Offstage are the bedroom and bathroom.

The Time: Not long ago. July.

Scene 1: Friday afternoon.
Scene 2: The following Tuesday afternoon.
Scene 3: The following Friday afternoon.

The play is meant to be performed without intermission.

A WORD FROM THE AUTHOR

Given the brevity of many lines in the script, actors may be inclined to "pick up the pace" and thereby reduce serious exchanges to trivial banter. The suggestion here is to resist that temptation and instead speak more deliberately, so as to communicate subtle insinuations and deeper feelings that underlie even seemingly casual dialogue.

Scene 1

(MELISSA's *apartment*)

(*July. Friday afternoon*)

(*The dining room table is set with plates, glasses, and silverware for two. Candlesticks and flowers suggest that a formal meal has been planned.*)

(DAVE, *sitting on the couch, checks his watch. He walks to the table, puts away a couple of pieces, then sits, sipping a drink.*)

(*The door opens, and* MELISSA *enters, carrying boxes and bags of newly purchased clothing. She shoves the door closed behind her.*)

MELISSA: Whoo! (*She lays down her packages.*) Murder out there!

(MELISSA *looks expectantly at* DAVE, *but he stares blankly. She removes her sunglasses and breathes deeply.*)

MELISSA: That heat is brutal!

(*As* DAVE *continues to stare,* MELISSA *removes her shoes.*)

MELISSA: Ohhhh, that feels good.

(*As* MELISSA *walks to the sofa,* DAVE *picks up his glass and walks silently past her to the kitchen.*)

MELISSA: Bring me a drink, will ya'?

(DAVE *pours a drink, then places it out of* MELISSA's *reach.*)

MELISSA: Over here!

(DAVE *gestures to the table setting.*)

MELISSA: I'm sorry I'm late, but—

DAVE: Three hours late.

MELISSA: Traffic was impossible! *(She retrieves the drink.)* Hope you didn't go to a lot of trouble.

(DAVE stares at MELISSA, then holds up a plate with food.)

MELISSA: I bet it was delicious.

DAVE: It would've been.

(DAVE noisily scrapes the food into the garbage. MELISSA watches with him.)

MELISSA: How can I make it up to you?

(MELISSA draws near DAVE, but he ducks away.)

DAVE: There you go again.

MELISSA: What?

DAVE: Leave me hanging, then apologize with "How can I make it up to you?" You do it every time.

MELISSA: At least I'm consistent.

DAVE: And who were you with?

MELISSA: I was trying on clothes—

DAVE: Who was there?

MELISSA: And I lost track of time!

DAVE: Who…was there?

(A beat)

MELISSA: Mickey.

DAVE: I knew it.

MELISSA: But that's his business! He even took me backstage to see the new lines!

DAVE: C'mon!

MELISSA: And it's gonna make a great story! *(A beat)* What can I say?

DAVE: I don't know. I don't even know what *I* can say. I'm totally…

MELISSA: Confused.

DAVE: Yes.

MELISSA: Befuddled.

DAVE: Maybe.

MELISSA: Baffled.

DAVE: I guess.

MELISSA: Buffaloed. *(A beat)* Confounded. *(A beat)* Flummoxed—

DAVE: Whatever!

(A beat)

MELISSA: Let's face it. We lead complicated lives.

DAVE: But it's always the same story. We make terrific plans, then half of 'em fall apart.

MELISSA: But the other half turn out fantastic.

DAVE: The greatest times of my life!

MELISSA: Because we're magic together! Concerts, movies, books. You know my tastes.

DAVE: In everything.

MELISSA: *(Laughing)* That's why I can't wait to get to the beach house next month. Mickey said it's a beautiful spot.

DAVE: How does he know—

MELISSA: He also wants to meet you.

DAVE: Why?

MELISSA: He's a fan.

DAVE: He's heard of me?

MELISSA: Not exactly, but he remembered *The Times* review.

DAVE: *(Intrigued)* He read the review?

MELISSA: No. But I quoted the blurb: "An incisive, graceful critique of a filmmaker too often neglected."

DAVE: You forgot "pellucid". "Incisive, *pellucid*, graceful."

MELISSA: And that's when he remembered that he's gonna buy the book.

DAVE: So he hasn't actually read it.

MELISSA: Then I told him about the film symposium in Philadelphia, how you left those clowns in your dust.

DAVE: *(Á la Bogart)* That's what I do, shweetheart.

MELISSA: And how I felt shivers all over. What I didn't tell him was about that night in the Hilton. How I felt shivers there, too.

DAVE: *(Á la Bogart)* We're good, shweetheart. Very good.

MELISSA: And when you started ladling out the Jell-O and whipped cream…

DAVE: *(Á la Bogart)* We'll alwaysh have Philadelphia.

MELISSA: I trust you'll bring an ample stock to the beach.

(A beat)

DAVE: And if I don't, I'm sure you'll find another supplier.

MELISSA: Awww…who could take your place?

DAVE: Are you kidding? I've seen so many men here… what about that construction worker?

MELISSA: Harry? C'mon! He's just a big friendly bear—

DAVE: Don't kid me!

MELISSA: Who happens to share my affection for hockey! I don't know what you imagine is going on—

DAVE: And the research technician. What about him?

MELISSA: Waldo? Little Waldo? Sweet little—

DAVE: You spent a whole night in his lab!

MELISSA: And that article was one of my best! *(A beat)* How can I make this all better?

DAVE: Are you really asking? Because you know the answer. *(He kneels and takes her hand.)* I want a commitment. Legal, binding for a lifetime. Two-ring ceremony. Throw the bouquet. Return the gifts. The works. I am ready to build a life together. Are you?

(A beat)

MELISSA: No.

DAVE: That didn't take much thought. *(He goes to the closet and removes a suitcase that he opens on the table.)*

MELISSA: What are you doing?

(DAVE opens the dresser, takes out clothes and brings them to the suitcase, then begins to pack them.)

MELISSA: C'mon, we can work this out. *(A beat)* Look, my career's finally taking off. I'm breaking through!

DAVE: And if you're married to me, you can't break through?

MELISSA: I have to be free to pick up and go. Anywhere! Any time!

DAVE: I won't stop you!

MELISSA: It wouldn't be the same.

DAVE: Fine. I am now declaring you free. Unshackled. You may go wherever the winds blow you—

MELISSA: Don't you see—

DAVE: Because I am leaving!

MELISSA: Wait!

(DAVE *stops*.)

MELISSA: I talked about you at the office the other day. Told them all about your writing and teaching. Even said you might win a fellowship for next year.

DAVE: Forget "might". I got it.

MELISSA: And the money?

DAVE: Every penny.

MELISSA: I am so proud of you! (*She kisses him, then turns away*.) But now we're finished. (*She turns back*.) Right?

DAVE: I don't know. I don't know anything. One minute you and I are together, and life couldn't be better. Then a minute later, you're off to God knows where, and I'm left...

(MELISSA *laughs softly*.)

DAVE: What?

MELISSA: Guess what I just remembered.

DAVE: I won't even try.

MELISSA: The first time we packed together. (*She wraps her hands in one of his shirts and holds it over her head*.) The first time you...you know what you did.

(DAVE *shrugs and smiles*.)

DAVE: Well...

MELISSA: I always liked this shirt.

DAVE: You picked it out.

MELISSA: I have wonderful taste, don't I?

DAVE: In shirts, yes.

MELISSA: I also picked you.

DAVE: One winner out of dozens.

(A beat)

MELISSA: Gonna miss you showing up every Thursday.

DAVE: You'll get over it. You always do.

MELISSA: Those four nights you're on the campus, I feel trapped in a cultural wasteland.

DAVE: Don't go overboard.

MELISSA: Overboard? Who won the Academy Award for Best Supporting Actor in 1985?

DAVE: What does that have to do with anything?

MELISSA: Never mind. Who won?

DAVE: 1985?

MELISSA: Best supporting actor.

DAVE: Don Ameche. *Cocoon.*

MELISSA: And how about Best Supporting Actress in 1955?

DAVE: Jo Van Fleet. *East of Eden.*

MELISSA: And who won the marathon in the 1952 Olympics?

DAVE: Why are you asking—

MELISSA: Answer the question!

DAVE: Emil Zatopek.

MELISSA: And that same year, who was the American League Batting Champion?

DAVE: Ferris Fain. Philadelphia A's. 327.

MELISSA: And what's the capital of the republic of Togo?

DAVE: Lomé. Now hold it! What is the point of—

MELISSA: The point is, how do you think I feel when we walk into a party, and you're my trivia partner? Have we ever lost?

DAVE: Of course not.

MELISSA: One more reason I love you.

DAVE: Love's a pretty strong word for winning a couple of board games.

MELISSA: Every time you leave, I try to put up a good front.

DAVE: You're very successful.

MELISSA: But inside I'm a mess. Helpless, lost—

DAVE: Then why is it every time I get home and call, you never pick up?

MELISSA: Depends on the day.

DAVE: Then I call again, and there's still no answer. In fact, it's turned off.

MELISSA: Sometimes when I'm down, I try to cheer myself up by being with other people.

DAVE: Male people.

MELISSA: Half the world's male, Dave.

DAVE: And you want to know 'em all.

MELISSA: Well, each one's good for something else.

DAVE: You have the most peculiar way of expressing yourself.

MELISSA: Take Bill.

DAVE: I'm sure you have.

MELISSA: Stop that. Now Bill knows Chinese food. He and I have probably eaten in every good Szechuan place in the city.

DAVE: No argument there.

MELISSA: And afterwards I've taken you to the best. That's how you get the benefit of my experience.

DAVE: Hold it—

MELISSA: Tommy loves to roller skate. Do you want to roller skate?

DAVE: You must be joking.

MELISSA: Tommy's crazy about it. So occasionally we hit the rink. What could be more innocent?

DAVE: Something must be.

MELISSA: Then there's… *(Rolling the "r")* UMBErrrto.

DAVE: *(Flat)* Umberto?

MELISSA: *(Extra rolling of the "r")* Um-*berrrr*-to—

DAVE: Who cares?

MELISSA: "Bertie" for short.

DAVE: Never mind! Who is he?

MELISSA: The man is a dancing fool.

DAVE: First time I've heard of him. Where did he—

MELISSA: We met at the racetrack.

DAVE: When?

MELISSA: When I was there with Brad.

DAVE: Who's *Brad?*

MELISSA: What's the difference? They like me. I like them.

DAVE: It's not that simple—

MELISSA: Because none of them…none of them compares to you. *(She brings her lips right to his, then breaks away.)* But now you're leaving.

DAVE: Don't you see that I want to be with you? All the time?

MELISSA: And there's another thing I love about you. You're my ballast, my lighthouse, my Rock of Gibraltar—

DAVE: Why do you sound like a song Cole Porter threw away?

MELISSA: You know what I mean. I can count on you.

DAVE: I'm here only three nights a week.

MELISSA: That's at least twice as often as anyone else.

DAVE: What's that supposed to mean?

MELISSA: It's a joke!

DAVE: When I'm at school, all I do is work.

MELISSA: You never see other women?

DAVE: Well...

MELISSA: Well...

DAVE: I see them.

MELISSA: And?

DAVE: But not with the zest that you see other men.

MELISSA: I have an extraordinary capacity for friendship.

DAVE: I've noticed. That's why I can't help wondering if any of these friendships ever become more...uhhh... complicated.

MELISSA: I'm not sure what you're saying.

DAVE: I'm not, either.

MELISSA: Because it sounds as if you don't trust me.

DAVE: I didn't say that!

MELISSA: But you did imply it.

DAVE: No, I didn't!

MELISSA: Good. Because whatever you think I'm doing with any of these guys—

DAVE: Okay.

MELISSA: Whatever antics you dream up—

DAVE: Okay! *(A beat)* The thing is…

MELISSA: Yes, what is "the thing?"

DAVE: The thing is…sometimes I wonder what's happening with you and…whoever, and that's when I want to know everything you're doing. But other times I don't want to know anything you're doing. But then I *do* want to know—

MELISSA: Dave, you must realize how special you are. Of all the men in my life…of all the men I know…of *all those men*…

DAVE: How many are there?

MELISSA: You are definitely the most important.

DAVE: Why is that thought less than comforting?

MELISSA: Guys fascinate me. They're fun to play with.

DAVE: What about me? Am I fun to play with?

MELISSA: The most! And remember, you're the only one who lives here. Regularly.

(DAVE stares at MELISSA.)

MELISSA: Joke!

DAVE: And what about settling down?

MELISSA: Not again.

DAVE: Do you ever consider it?

MELISSA: All the time.

DAVE: I mean with me.

MELISSA: Who else?

DAVE: And?

MELISSA: You know what happens. Two people who have great single lives get married, and suddenly problems pop up everywhere. I don't want that to happen to us.

DAVE: We're not like other couples.

MELISSA: That's what every couple says.

DAVE: Besides, we know each other so well. What are you afraid of? What problems could we possibly have?

MELISSA: You want me to name the problems?

DAVE: I want to hear them.

MELISSA: Really?

DAVE: Really.

MELISSA: All right. *(A beat)* Where do we live? Here? Your place?

DAVE: Well, we have several possibilities—

MELISSA: And they're all bad.

DAVE: I didn't say that—

MELISSA: And who's taking care of this imaginary paradise?

DAVE: There'll be two of us.

MELISSA: That's another thing.

DAVE: Why?

MELISSA: We'll have to choose furniture and décor, we'll have to fix and clean—

DAVE: But this is all little stuff!

MELISSA: Little? How can someone so smart be so stupid? Let's start with the fact that I prefer hardwood floors, and you hate them.

DAVE: I don't hate them—

MELISSA: Would you still insist on laying that atrocious shag carpet?

DAVE: I think it looks classy, but again, we can discuss it—

MELISSA: I don't want to discuss it. I like it my way. And how about the mattress that's perfect for me, but that you claim is like sleeping on "bed...rock"?

DAVE: I can get used to anything.

MELISSA: The way you're used to finding my hair on the soap?

DAVE: Oh, well, that's particularly...

MELISSA: Gross?

DAVE: Not the word I would have chosen.

MELISSA: Then how about the used cotton balls floating in the toilet?

DAVE: No problem. I've learned to deal with your... sanitary souvenirs.

MELISSA: Or the ever-popular toothpaste without the cap on? Marriages explode over less.

DAVE: We just have to be considerate of each other.

MELISSA: You mean I have to be considerate of you.

DAVE: Not at all—

MELISSA: Will you ever stop complaining that I leave my flip-flops in the living room? Or that I go for weeks without changing the sheets on my bed?

DAVE: Those are just charming quirks—

MELISSA: And if you lived here every day, you still think they'd be charming?

DAVE: I hereby accept responsibility for bed-making and footwear. *(He picks up her shoes)* Where would you like these?

(When MELISSA *points,* DAVE *drops the shoes there.)*

DAVE: Nothing to it.

(DAVE kisses MELISSA.)

MELISSA: Will you also let me buy the toilet paper I like?

DAVE: I have explained many times that two-ply is not only sturdier, but costs less—

MELISSA: Then use it at your house. I like my brand.

DAVE: But if you'd just listen—

MELISSA: Yours feels like I'm cleaning myself with a marshmallow. And even though I've told you a hundred times, you still insist on bringing it into *my* apartment!

DAVE: All right. Okay. I can see how that can be irritating. I'll keep my opinion to myself.

MELISSA: And how about when I drink milk past the expiration date? Or use extra-chunky blue cheese dressing?

(DAVE *grimaces in pain.*)

MELISSA: Or eat salted peanuts—

DAVE: They're bad for you!

MELISSA: I like 'em!

DAVE: Yeah, but—

MELISSA: I like them!

DAVE: Okay, but—

MELISSA: Right now, when you're around, I put 'em away. I won't do that forever.

DAVE: No?

MELISSA: No! Because I like 'em! *(Short pause)* Getting the idea?

DAVE: Yeah, yeah. But I still say that whatever happens, we'll have one compromise, one agreement after another.

MELISSA: That apartment might get small.

DAVE: Apartment? Aren't we going to live in a house?

MELISSA: There aren't many houses in Manhattan—

DAVE: But I teach in New Jersey.

MELISSA: But my base is the city. And that minor difference might create a "problem."

DAVE: Forget it. I'll be fine. Because I'll be with you. And you're wonderful.

MELISSA: But why should force ourselves—

DAVE: Forget it! Next problem.

MELISSA: Okay. *(A beat)* How about money? Who's in charge?

DAVE: We're a team. Co-captains.

MELISSA: And if you want to spend, and I don't? Or the other way around?

DAVE: Whatever I have is yours. Next problem.

MELISSA: You can't imagine disagreements of any kind?

DAVE: Oh, I can imagine them. But I can also imagine that we'll work them out.

MELISSA: Uh-huh. What about sex?

DAVE: What about it? We're glorious together, right?

MELISSA: I must admit—

DAVE: Right! Okay, maybe, *maybe* an occasional moment of awkwardness. But we can handle it.

MELISSA: Nice turn of phrase.

DAVE: Never mind that. Next problem.

MELISSA: Okay. Let's take something that really matters. Do you want children?

DAVE: Eventually.

MELISSA: There's another problem.

DAVE: Why? Don't you want a family?

MELISSA: I don't know. That's why it's a problem.

DAVE: I'm not talking about right away. I mean one day.

MELISSA: I still don't know.

DAVE: Well, we have time to decide. But why—

MELISSA: When?

DAVE: When what? When are we going to decide? Or when are we going to have 'em?

MELISSA: Either.

DAVE: I'm not sure. We'll discuss it.

MELISSA: Hm-mm. And how many?

DAVE: We'll discuss that as well.

MELISSA: Suppose I say two.

DAVE: Then we'll discuss it and decide.

MELISSA: Is that your solution to everything? Discuss it?

DAVE: I think it's called acting like grown-ups.

MELISSA: But it isn't that easy.

DAVE: I never said it would be. All I'm saying is that we make each other incredibly happy. And if there's something better than finding someone who makes you happy, I haven't heard about it.

MELISSA: Then let's say that after all this discussion, we decide to have two children.

DAVE: Sounds good. End of problem.

MELISSA: Not exactly. We now have two children.

DAVE: So?

MELISSA: I repeat: two children. Who get sick, who throw tantrums, who have problems of their own, and who grow up to have even worse problems.

DAVE: I know what you're saying. But to me it all sounds like...a challenge. Not a problem.

MELISSA: A very big challenge.

DAVE: But think of the rewards. Think of all the parents who look at their kids with pride, who can say that all the time and effort was...okay, it's a big challenge. But I can see 'em right now. Two great kids. And we're all piling into the car...okay, it's a very big challenge. But we can do it.

MELISSA: And who stays home with them?

DAVE: Am I domestic or not? And remember, I set my own class schedule.

MELISSA: What about families? In-laws?

DAVE: What about 'em? My folks are nice. Most of the time.

MELISSA: Really? I can't stand listening to your father ask every ten minutes when you'll teach a course on Popeye the sailor.

DAVE: He's just joking—

MELISSA: And you hate his jokes as much as I do.

DAVE: Well, every family has difficulties. I mean, look at your sister. You can barely be in the same room with her! And that cousin. What's his name? Ronald.

MELISSA: Rodney. Exactly. They're unbearable! Put them all together, and we won't survive the wedding! *(She mimes an explosion.)* Psshew!

DAVE: Well...

MELISSA: Right now we're single, so we don't have to go anywhere.

DAVE: And that's good, isn't it?

MELISSA: But once we're a couple, they'll expect us to go everywhere. And we'll hate it.

DAVE: But couldn't we—

MELISSA: No, we couldn't. And so far we've hit only the obvious traps. Think about everything we haven't mentioned!

DAVE: I know, but—

MELISSA: The way things stand, we have a terrific time. No one makes me as happy as you do.

DAVE: And nothing makes me happier than making you happy.

MELISSA: We're the happiest non-couple I know. We have our connection. But we also have our freedom. And our fun!

DAVE: Great, but—

MELISSA: We're on a terrific ride!

DAVE: That's how I feel!

MELISSA: Then why jump off the merry-go-round?

(Short pause)

DAVE: Because I need more. And no matter how many miserable pictures you draw, I still want it.

MELISSA: Even though we might ruin everything.

DAVE: I'm willing to bet on us. Are you?

(A beat)

MELISSA: Not yet. And that's why I'm asking you to be patient.

DAVE: Until . . .?

MELISSA: One day.

DAVE: And then?

MELISSA: I'll let you know.

DAVE: When do you think that might be?

(MELISSA *kisses* DAVE.)

MELISSA: Okay?

(A beat)

DAVE: One request?

MELISSA: Name it.

DAVE: Have a little less fun when I'm not around.

MELISSA: That's cute. *(She kisses him.)* Great to have you back.

DAVE: Great to be had.

(MELISSA *goes to the suitcase, takes out some clothes, and dumps them in the drawer.)*

DAVE: Hey! I have to wear those.

(MELISSA *dumps out the rest and takes the suitcase to the closet.)*

MELISSA: Not tonight.

DAVE: Yeah, but tomorrow I have—

(MELISSA *closes the closet door.)*

MELISSA: I'm not thinking about tomorrow. And tonight you won't be wearing much of anything.

(MELISSA *walks over slowly and kisses* DAVE. *He responds tentatively.)*

MELISSA: Help a little.

(DAVE *responds passionately.)*

MELISSA: Isn't this the best?

DAVE: I never said it wasn't.

MELISSA: And are we back to normal?

DAVE: Whatever that means.

MELISSA: Gonna to stay forever and ever?

DAVE: 'Til Sunday, anyway.

MELISSA: Perfect. Monday I have a date with Leo.

DAVE: What?

MELISSA: Just a yoga class. Relax!

DAVE: Aren't you ever going to change?

MELISSA: I hope not. Now. What do we want for dinner? What would you like?

DAVE: Let's not bother with Chinese. That's Bill's territory.

MELISSA: Right, I get that all the time. Anyway, while you're deciding, how'd you like a fashion show?

(*As* DAVE *scurries to the sofa,* MELISSA *picks up the packages.*)

MELISSA: I just bought these for the beach. Skimpy, tiny little things.

(MELISSA *opens a box and gives it to* DAVE, *who pulls out part of a bikini.*)

MELISSA: Were you going to say something?

DAVE: Only that I'd love to see them.

(MELISSA *smiles and starts for the bedroom. The telephone rings. As she puts down the boxes and goes to answer it,* DAVE *plays with the bikini part.*)

MELISSA: Hold that thought. Hello? (*A beat*) Well, hi, stranger! Where've you been? (*A beat*) Just fine! (*She settles on the sofa.*) Oh, you know. Assignments all over. (*A beat*) Did you see that one? Well, thank you very much.

(*Sitting next to* MELISSA, DAVE *tries to distract her with the bikini. She ignores him.*)

MELISSA: Now tell me: what's going on?

(DAVE *pokes* MELISSA. *She wriggles.*)

MELISSA: No, this is fine. Go ahead.

(DAVE's *pokes* MELISSA *again. She laughs and pushes his hand away.*)

MELISSA: And what happened?

(*The poking turns into tickling.* MELISSA *slaps* DAVE's *hand away.*)

MELISSA: Great!

(DAVE *continues to poke and tickle.* MELISSA *laughs loudly and pushes him away.*)

MELISSA: Nothing! You just always make me laugh! What time? (*A beat*) And where? (*Still laughing and squirming*) Okay! If I can make it! 'Bye!

(MELISSA *tosses away the phone and pushes* DAVE *away.*)

MELISSA: What is the matter with you?

DAVE: I trust that wasn't anything important.

MELISSA: You were so rude I shouldn't even say.

DAVE: Fine.

MELISSA: Although it does involve you.

DAVE: Me? How?

(MELISSA *curls up next to* DAVE.)

MELISSA: You'll never guess who that was.

DAVE: I never can.

MELISSA: Actually, you don't know him. His name's Brian. And he's an old friend.

DAVE: Aren't they all.

MELISSA: Used to be a stockbroker.

DAVE: Was he arrested?

MELISSA: No, no. Just got tired of the rat race.

DAVE: Well, I'm sure running on that little wheel can be exhausting—

MELISSA: Then he became a forest ranger. But that didn't work out, either.

DAVE: Got tired of trees?

MELISSA: Then he was a sculptor. Then a writer. And then an actor.

DAVE: I knew we'd get there eventually.

MELISSA: Even tried to be a comedian.

DAVE: Powerhouse résumé.

MELISSA: Then he hit it big.

DAVE: Don't tell me. He sells drugs.

MELISSA: No! He started a health club. And he did so well that we have plans for tonight.

DAVE: I don't see the logic.

MELISSA: He's opening a new gym, and we're invited.

DAVE: *We* are.

MELISSA: Well, not you. But I'm sure everyone would be thrilled to have you there.

DAVE: What'll I be? Your personal dumbbell?

MELISSA: Something wrong?

DAVE: Let me get this straight. After our entire discussion, after all the fuss about how I feel, one phone call, and you're off for the evening?

MELISSA: Think of the people we'll meet!

DAVE: At a gym? I have very little interest in meeting anyone whose mission in life is to sweat!

MELISSA: If I know Brian well...and I surely do...he'll have a celebrity clientele. We're going to make contacts tonight.

DAVE: Maybe, but—

MELISSA: If you want to stay here by yourself, that's up to you. But I'd really like you with me.

DAVE: You mean you're definitely going?

MELISSA: It'll be fun!

(A beat)

DAVE: Suppose I asked you not to go.

MELISSA: Why would you do that?

DAVE: Because all week I have been dreaming of being here with you. In fact, the only reason I visit the city is to be with you. I'm very happy in New Jersey.

MELISSA: Speaking for the city, we are delighted any time you join us.

DAVE: But suppose I said that I'm not going under any circumstances, and I don't want you to go either.

MELISSA: You wouldn't.

DAVE: Why not?

MELISSA: Because that would make me unhappy, and you could never do that.

DAVE: Twenty minutes ago I was leaving this place.

MELISSA: You're still here.

DAVE: I was ready to leave.

MELISSA: No, you weren't.

DAVE: I was packing!

MELISSA: Not really.

DAVE: You saw me, didn't you? You saw me putting my clothes in a suitcase.

MELISSA: It was an act. You'd never leave.

DAVE: You mean, if I said that if you go to that gym tonight I'll leave, you wouldn't believe me?

MELISSA: I told you—

DAVE: Do you think I am so weak-willed, so lacking in pride—

MELISSA: Not at all.

DAVE: Do you think I am such a chump—

MELISSA: No. You're just not leaving.

DAVE: You think so.

MELISSA: I know so.

DAVE: You wanna bet?

MELISSA: Sure.

DAVE: You want to make a bet that I will not leave today.

MELISSA: If you want.

DAVE: That I will not take that same suitcase out of that same closet, open that same dresser, and put away those same clothes? You really want to make that bet?

MELISSA: Hm-mm.

DAVE: You're on! What are the stakes?

MELISSA: If I win, we go to the opening tonight.

DAVE: And if I win?

MELISSA: Name it.

(A beat)

DAVE: I don't know. Let me think.

MELISSA: Anything you want.

DAVE: We have to agree first.

MELISSA: No, we don't. I'll agree right now. If you pack and walk out, I'll do anything you want.

DAVE: Are you serious?

MELISSA: Perfectly.

DAVE: Anything I want?

MELISSA: Anything.

DAVE: Even…that thing we saw in the magazine last week?

MELISSA: Any…thing.

(A beat)

DAVE: It's a bet.

MELISSA: Good. Let's kiss on it.

DAVE: No way. Let's just get started.

MELISSA: Go ahead.

DAVE: All right! *(He points to the closet.)* I am going to the closet.

MELISSA: Good for you.

(DAVE reaches the closet. MELISSA moves sensuously to the sofa.)

DAVE: I am now opening the door of the closet. *(He opens the door.)* …taking out the suitcase… *(He takes out the suitcase.)* …and bringing it to the table… *(He brings the suitcase to the table.)* …where I shall now begin to pack. Are you watching?

MELISSA: Every step.

(DAVE goes to the dresser. MELISSA stretches out.)

DAVE: I am now taking my clothes out of the dresser.

(DAVE brings some clothes over. MELISSA stretches seductively. He notices.)

DAVE: You're not getting to me. Not this time. *(He turns and hurries to the dresser.)* I can do this.

MELISSA: *(Moaning)* D-a-a-a-ve.

DAVE: I'm busy. *(He piles in more clothes.)*

MELISSA: *(Stretching and moaning)* D-a-a-a-a-a-ave.

DAVE: What?

(MELISSA *beckons to* DAVE.)

DAVE: No.

(MELISSA *beckons.*)

DAVE: I'm not coming over.

MELISSA: I want to talk to you.

DAVE: I'm not coming over. And you can't make me.

MELISSA: But I want to talk to you.

(DAVE *looks at* MELISSA. *She beckons.*)

MELISSA: Just for me. Please?

(*A beat*)

DAVE: For one minute.

MELISSA: That's all I want.

(DAVE *walks tentatively to* MELISSA. *He sits on the sofa, as far from her as possible.*)

MELISSA: Let me say one thing.

(MELISSA *runs her foot up and down* DAVE's *arm. He pushes her foot away.*)

DAVE: I'm packing. After you say whatever it is you want to say, I am packing. Then I'm leaving.

(MELISSA *runs her foot along* DAVE's *leg.*)

MELISSA: Shhh.

(*As* DAVE *starts to stand,* MELISSA *pulls him back.*)

DAVE: Won't do any good.

(MELISSA *kneels on the sofa and puts her finger to* DAVE's *lips.*)

MELISSA: Shhhhhh.

DAVE: Forget it.

MELISSA: But I want you to know something.

DAVE: You can say anything you want, but I'm leaving.

MELISSA: I care for you very much.

DAVE: I'm not buying it.

MELISSA: You are a special man and a special part of my life.

DAVE: That may be, but—

MELISSA: And there's something else.

DAVE: Go ahead. I can take it.

(MELISSA *puts her arms around* DAVE'*s neck.)*

MELISSA: You are…without a doubt…the best I have ever had.

(DAVE *stares at* MELISSA, *then laughs.)*

DAVE: Are you serious? Do you think you can bring out a line like that and fool me?

(MELISSA *strokes* DAVE'*s face.)*

DAVE: That line is so old…there is not a man in the world who believes it. Not one. No, sir.

MELISSA: But it's true.

DAVE: Won't work. No way.

MELISSA: No one has ever made me feel so warm. So loved.

DAVE: There's no use—

MELISSA: You are…masterful.

(Short pause)

DAVE: All right. Let's say it is true. You still won't get me.

MELISSA: I'm not finished.

DAVE: Won't do any good—

MELISSA: I want you here. Because you love me.

DAVE: Of course I do! That's what this is all about!

MELISSA: Then say it.

DAVE: I have very deep feelings for you—

MELISSA: Say it.

DAVE: Fine. I love you.

(DAVE *and* MELISSA *kiss passionately. He breaks away.*)

DAVE: *(Breathless)* But that doesn't mean I'm a pushover.

MELISSA: Of course not. *(She puts some of his clothes back in the dresser.)*

DAVE: Don't do that. I'll only take them out again!

MELISSA: Not today. *(She transfers more clothes.)*

DAVE: Oh, no, no, no, no! We have a bet!

(DAVE *tries to block* MELISSA, *but she moves him aside.*)

DAVE: I'm telling you. I'm putting them right back in—

MELISSA: Not today. *(She takes the rest of the clothes from the suitcase.)*

DAVE: But what about the bet? I wanna win the bet.

(MELISSA *closes the empty suitcase and puts it in the closet.*)

MELISSA: Forget the bet. Just stay with me, and I'm yours.

DAVE: And what does that mean?

MELISSA: Think of the best time we've ever had. The absolute peak. Now double it. Triple it. That's what we'll have tonight.

DAVE: But if I win the bet, I get anything I want.

MELISSA: But it's only good for tonight. If you win and you leave, how will you collect?

DAVE: Well, I'll just…

MELISSA: But if you stay, I'm yours.

DAVE: But I lose the bet.

MELISSA: But you win me.

DAVE: But I'll have to go to that stupid gym.

MELISSA: But when you come back, I'll be here. And whatever you dream, that's what we'll do.

(DAVE *reflects.*)

DAVE: You really want me here?

MELISSA: More than anything.

DAVE: Then suppose you had a choice. Either you stay here tonight with me, in which case I also stay. Or you go to that gym, and I leave. One or the other. You go, and I leave. You stay, and I stay. Which do you choose?

MELISSA: Simple. Whatever will make us both happy.

(MELISSA *kisses* DAVE. *Short pause)*

DAVE: I lost the bet, didn't I?

MELISSA: Hm-mm. Do you care?

(A beat)

DAVE: No.

MELISSA: Good. Now let's get dressed. We have a big night ahead. *(She turns to go into the bedroom.)*

DAVE: One second.

(MELISSA *turns around.)*

DAVE: You say that I'm the most important man in your life.

MELISSA: No question about it.

DAVE: How do I know that you don't tell that to any other guys?

MELISSA: You don't. *(A beat)* You just have to trust me.

(MELISSA *smiles, turns back to the bedroom and leaves.* DAVE *stares quizzically.)*

(End of Scene 1)

Scene 2

(The following Tuesday afternoon)

(The doorbell rings. MELISSA, *dressed stylishly for business, checks her appearance.)*

(The bell rings again. She goes to the door and opens it to find BETH.)

BETH: Melissa?

MELISSA: Right. And you must be Beth.

BETH: That's me! *(She enters.)*

MELISSA: C'mon in.

BETH: Thanks *so* much! It is *so* nice to meet you after all this time.

(BETH *offers her hand.* MELISSA *shakes it awkwardly.)*

MELISSA: You, too.

BETH: Oh, you don't have to say that! But thanks anyway!

(MELISSA *closes the door.)*

MELISSA: Not at all. I'm afraid my schedule is a bit tight this afternoon—

BETH: Oh, I understand! David says you're always involved with somebody somewhere. *(She drops her handbag on the sofa.)*

MELISSA: Just part of the job.

BETH: Of course! I'm lucky you're seeing me at all! But since I had to drop off that manuscript, I decided—

MELISSA: You told me—

BETH: That as long as I was going to be in town, I'd give you a ring!

MELISSA: And I'm glad you did.

BETH: Thanks *so* much! But whenever you have to leave, just tell me, and I'll scoot!

MELISSA: Well, actually—

BETH: And this apartment looks *just* the way I imagined! David told me that you had good taste, but this is just lovely!

MELISSA: Thank you. Would you like to sit?

BETH: Do you mind if I walk a while? The bus ride was *so* uncomfortable. All cramped and crowded. Do you mind?

MELISSA: Whatever you like.

BETH: Thanks *so* much! *(She strolls, looking carefully.)*

MELISSA: Something to drink?

BETH: I don't want to bother you.

MELISSA: It's no bother—

BETH: But it is really hot out there!

MELISSA: What would you like?

BETH: Something very light!

MELISSA: Pepsi?

BETH: Could you make that Diet Pepsi?

MELISSA: Comin' up.

BETH: Thanks *so* much!

*(*MELISSA *goes to the refrigerator.)*

BETH: It's not as bad in the country as it is here. But it's sticky out there, too. And buggy!

MELISSA: All those tree and ponds, I suppose.

(MELISSA *brings* BETH *the drink.*)

BETH: You think? *(She accepts the drink.)* Thanks so much! *(She sips.)* Oh! That's marvelous! That bus was unbearable! I guess the air conditioning wasn't working, because they opened the windows, but even so, it was stifling! And the seats were so…so…

MELISSA: Sticky?

BETH: Right! And the wind was blowing in my face. I must look a mess! *(She looks into an imaginary mirror in the audience and fixes her hair.)*

MELISSA: Not at all.

BETH: I know I do, but that's so nice of you! *(A beat)* By the way, you are just as pretty as David said.

MELISSA: Thank you.

BETH: And that outfit is terrific!

MELISSA: You're very kind.

BETH: Y' know, I have to tell you. Today is a treat for me. I mean, I get to the city so rarely, 'cause I have to be in the office every day.

(As BETH *and* MELISSA *stand near each other,* BETH *measures her foot against* MELISSA'*s.* MELISSA *moves to the sofa.)*

MELISSA: Don't you want to sit?

BETH: In a minute. I'll just look around, okay?

MELISSA: Up to you.

BETH: Thanks!

(As BETH *walks around,* MELISSA *watches her.)*

MELISSA: Exactly what do you do in the office?

BETH: Officially I'm an administrative associate, but that's just a fancy word for secretary. Plus I'm also a student.

MELISSA: And how did you get to know David?

BETH: You mean how did we meet? Or how did we become friends?

(A beat)

MELISSA: I mean, how did you get to know him?

BETH: Oh! *(She laughs.)* Well, from the day I entered the program, I heard how great he was. Then last fall I took one of his courses, and this past spring two more. But it was that first one that really got me: "Films of the Thirties". One of his specialties, you know.

MELISSA: I know.

BETH: *(Lascivious)* Just one of them! *(She laughs.)* Guess I've always been a movie buff. I'll see anything! Do you know anyone like that?

MELISSA: I do now.

BETH: So when I found out I could get a graduate degree in, quote, cinema studies, how could I resist?

MELISSA: How indeed.

BETH: And that first course *was great*. Some John Ford, some of the screwball comedies, a couple of gangster things. *(She suddenly mimes James Cagney and gives a feeble impression of his voice.)* "You dirty rat!"

(BETH pauses, then laughs. MELISSA scurries away.)

MELISSA: Very good.

BETH: The whole thing was a kick. But I'm sure I don't have to tell you the best part.

MELISSA: The best film, you mean?

BETH: The best part of the course.

MELISSA: What was that?

BETH: You mean I really have to tell you?

MELISSA: Oh.

BETH: The first time I heard him I was taken.

MELISSA: That's understandable.

BETH: *(Dreamily)* Yeah. When he talks about movies...
excuse me, *film*...

MELISSA: I prefer "movies".

BETH: You know what? So does David! *(She laughs.)*

MELISSA: I know.

BETH: Anyway, when he talks, you feel so much...
knowledge, so much experience—

MELISSA: He's quite good.

BETH: "Quite good"! Is that all?

MELISSA: He's excellent.

BETH: Just amazing!

MELISSA: Amazing. That's what I mean.

BETH: *(Sitting on the sofa)* I think he's seen every movie
that matters, and read all the books and articles.

MELISSA: He's done beautifully.

BETH: Inspiring. That's what he is. *(She takes out a comb
and brushes her hair.)*

MELISSA: Just amazing.

BETH: Have you ever seen him in class?

MELISSA: No, I—

BETH: Take it from me. He's dynamite! I can't believe
his family wanted him to stay in the appliance
business.

MELISSA: I've heard—

BETH: I know the money'd be great, but a man should do what he wants, right?

MELISSA: I suppose so—

BETH: And of course he is simply so funny!

MELISSA: He is?

BETH: A clown! I don't think we ever stop laughing. And hardly a class goes by that he doesn't give us at least one giant guffaw.

MELISSA: Fundamentally, though, he's a serious guy. *(She sits on the sofa.)*

BETH: You think so? Then you don't know him as well as I thought.

(A beat)

MELISSA: Perhaps I see a different side—

BETH: When was the last time he took you dancing?

MELISSA: Not…recently.

BETH: The first time we went, I couldn't believe it.

MELISSA: He was a klutz.

BETH: He was dynamite! *(She laughs.)* That seems to be the word of the day, right? But whenever I describe David, that's the one that comes to mind.

MELISSA: Dynamite.

BETH: You, too, huh? *(A beat)* At first he didn't want to go. I mean, he really didn't want to go! But I worked on him. And before I knew it, he was spinning me around the floor. Turned into a party animal. But that can't surprise you.

MELISSA: A bit, perhaps—

BETH: That's another reason I go for him. He just… does things! Like one day we were hanging around his office, and it was really nice outside, one of those great spring days. The sun was shining, and it was warm and breezy, when all of a sudden he said, "Let's go on a picnic!" And before I had a chance to think, he took me by the hand, and off we went. He whipped up some sandwiches...you know how handy he is... and bingo! There we were, sitting on a blanket in the middle of the park, eating and drinking. Like something out of *Wuthering Heights*. The man is a constant surprise!

MELISSA: He's a caution.

(BETH *sits close to* MELISSA.)

BETH: Do you mind if I talk personally?

MELISSA: Why not?

BETH: Thanks *so* much! Well, pretty soon I began to think about him more seriously. After all, he and I share almost everything. Our careers match. We both like living in the country. We both have a touch of the madcap. And we're compatible in...other ways. If you know what I mean.

MELISSA: I think I do.

BETH: Right. And a man who likes to cook? Is that great or is that great?

MELISSA: Sounds awfully good.

BETH: So I put all this together, and what I have is one heckuva guy. And even though professors don't make the biggest salaries...well, he may not have gone into the family business, but he's enjoying his share of the family portfolio. And someday he'll get a lot more.

MELISSA: You've certainly thought things through.

BETH: If I don't look out for me, who will?

MELISSA: Well said.

BETH: Thanks *so* much! Anyway, a couple of months ago matters became really interesting.

MELISSA: And why is that?

BETH: Because that's when I asked…if I could move in with him! *(A beat. She laughs.)*

MELISSA: Direct, aren't you?

BETH: Uh-huh. And guess what he said.

MELISSA: I have no idea.

BETH: Go ahead. Guess!

MELISSA: I don't want to guess.

(A beat)

BETH: He said no.

MELISSA: I'm so sorry.

(MELISSA takes BETH's hand.)

BETH: Thanks. *(She takes MELISSA's hand.)* I don't mind admitting that I was hurt.

MELISSA: Understandable.

BETH: But not for long. I just realized that I wasn't the only woman in his life, and he didn't want to be tied down. Besides, he has all those dates on campus, right?

(A beat)

MELISSA: Right.

BETH: But I couldn't believe that was all. So a week later I asked him again. Could I move in? And what do you think he said this time?

MELISSA: I don't know.

BETH: Guess.

(MELISSA stares at BETH.)

BETH: He still said no. But this time he told me about you.

MELISSA: Good for him.

BETH: Not everything, of course, because all he told me was that he stayed with someone in New York. But gradually he opened up.

MELISSA: Exactly what did he say?

BETH: Only the nicest things! Don't worry!

MELISSA: I won't.

BETH: Good! Anyway, I didn't mind. He's entitled to his life. And I was having such a wonderful time with him, if only for a couple of days each week. But now that's become a problem. And all because he is crazy about you!

MELISSA: Did he say that?

BETH: No. But a girl always knows, right? *(A beat)* That's why I'll bet you're wondering why I'm here.

MELISSA: As a matter of fact—

BETH: I knew it! *(She laughs and begins to walk.)* Well, let me explain. At first, I just wanted to see you. After all, I've heard so much about you that…well, I thought you and I ought to talk.

MELISSA: Does David know you're here?

BETH: Oh, no! He didn't even give me your address. But I managed to find the telephone number, and then…you know.

MELISSA: Aren't you resourceful!

BETH: Thanks! Now. How can I put this? *(A beat)* I'm interested in him. Very, very interested. To put it right on the line, I want to marry him. *(A beat)* And you're in the way! *(She laughs.)* There! I said it! You don't mind my coming right out like that, do you? After all, we're both women. And he's just a man, right? *(She laughs.)*

It's up to us to decide these things. Why should we have secrets?

MELISSA: No reason at all.

BETH: You know, you're just as sweet as David says! *(She stands.)* And just as pretty! Oh, I said that already!

MELISSA: Thank you—

BETH: But, then, I'm adorable. *(Short pause)* You don't have to say anything. I know it.

MELISSA: No argument here.

BETH: Thanks *so* much! *(She holds up her glass.)* Should I put this in the sink?

MELISSA: That would be fine.

BETH: My pleasure. *(She deposits the glass.)*

MELISSA: As long as we're being honest—

BETH: Forgive me, but I have to ask one thing.

MELISSA: Go ahead.

BETH: It's personal.

MELISSA: The floor is yours.

BETH: You are *so* nice! *(A beat)* David always tells me how beautifully you dress. Could I...look in your closet?

MELISSA: *(Laughing)* I beg your pardon?

BETH: *(Laughing)* I know it's terribly rude, but...could I peek? Just for half a sec?

MELISSA: I don't usually allow anybody to peek anywhere—

BETH: I'm sure you don't, but would you mind?

MELISSA: Well, if you really want—

BETH: Oh, wow! Thanks! *(She opens the closet.)* My goodness! What an assortment! *(She examines the clothing, then takes out couple of dresses and lays them down.)* And what an eye for color!

MELISSA: Thank you!

(AS BETH *puts the outfits down,* MELISSA *scrambles to re-hang them.)*

MELISSA: If you don't mind—

*(*BETH *takes out another dress and holds it up.)*

BETH: This…is…stunning! *(She presses the dress against herself.)* I hate to ask…I mean, you've been so great and all…but would you mind…could I please…?

MELISSA: Try it on?

BETH: Thanks *so* much!

MELISSA: No, I didn't mean—

BETH: You're the best! *(She steps out of her shoes, and begins to remove her clothes and put on* MELISSA*'s dress.)*

MELISSA: But I'd rather you didn't—

BETH: I won't take a minute!

MELISSA: It's not the time—

BETH: Isn't this the most fun?

MELISSA: Well, that depends—

BETH: David tells me you're a journalist.

MELISSA: Right. Uhhh… *(She pours herself a drink.)*

BETH: I really admire people with a creative spark. But that job must keep you hopping. How do you find time to think about anyone else?

MELISSA: Not easy—

BETH: David's told me that sometimes you can barely squeeze him in. *(She has the dress on. She straightens herself.)*

MELISSA: I'm not sure that'll fit.

BETH: But at least I'll get an idea. Let me check the mirror, okay? She flounces to the mirror, then checks herself.) I'll say it again. You have a great eye!

MELISSA: Thank you—

BETH: I only wish I were mature enough to wear something like this. (A beat) Of course, it's a couple of sizes too big for me. But it must look great on you.

MELISSA: It works out.

BETH: I bet it does. (She turns to MELISSA.) I bet it does.

(A beat)

MELISSA: Can we please move on?

BETH: Of course! I'd try on all day if I could. (She laughs and takes off the dress.)

MELISSA: I can tell—

BETH: There's nothing I enjoy more! (The dress is off.) Except David. (She re-hangs the dress.) That was fun. Thanks so much! (She looks inside the closet.) You know what?

MELISSA: I really don't.

BETH: With all this heat, I'd like to let my own clothes air out. (She pulls a man's dress shirt from the closet.) Mind if I slip this on?

MELISSA: I'm not sure David would approve—

BETH: Oh, he wouldn't care. Besides, he'll never know. (She puts it on. It is too large.) I love wearing a man's shirt. Makes me feel as if he was cuddling me right in his arms. (She sniffs a sleeve.) And I adore David's cologne! Mmmmm! I've known other men who wear it. But somehow on him, it's special.

(BETH lies on the sofa. Short pause)

MELISSA: You still haven't explained why you're here.

BETH: Haven't I?

MELISSA: So why don't you start now?

(BETH *sits up.*)

BETH: Okay! *(A beat)* What we have here might be called sort of a...predicament. You live with him. I want to live with him.

MELISSA: Is that it?

BETH: We both like him. We both enjoy...other men.

MELISSA: Does he know that?

BETH: Does it matter? *(A beat)* The question is...where do we go from here?

MELISSA: Why do we have to go anywhere? Why don't we leave the predicament as is?

BETH: So we each get the best of both worlds?

MELISSA: I wouldn't put it that way, but—

BETH: After all, he provides home cooking. And a regular, reliable partner in bed.

MELISSA: Agreed.

BETH: Plus he gives us opportunity for recreation.

MELISSA: You are direct.

BETH: Then we understand each other.

MELISSA: So what's the problem?

BETH: I'm afraid all that isn't good enough anymore.

MELISSA: Why not?

BETH: Because I want to settle down. I want something full-time, seven days a week, forever. I know it sounds old-fashioned, but I guess the ol' nesting instinct is taking over. Don't worry. I want my career, but I want everything else, too. That's not selfish, is it?

MELISSA: I wouldn't say so.

BETH: And of all the men I know, David's the one
I want most. He's not ideal, but before long I'll be
teaching, and we'll be able to share vacations, a nice
house, and all the other benefits of a substantial
inheritance. So what can I say? He's number one in my
book. How about you?

MELISSA: How about me, what?

BETH: Where does he rate with you?

MELISSA: Very high. He's not ideal, as you say, but…

BETH: He offers a lot.

(A beat)

MELISSA: Right.

BETH: Well, I think you'd better be a little more
definite. And soon.

MELISSA: How soon?

BETH: Couple of weeks.

MELISSA: Doesn't give me much time.

BETH: What can I say?

(A beat)

MELISSA: Exactly what is the rush? Are you threatening
to walk in and—

BETH: Oh, no, no, no! Do you think I could steal him
away from you? Not a chance.

MELISSA: Then what?

BETH: I just think he's ready to settle down, too.
He's fooled around long enough. Now he's looking
for…what I'm looking for. And the sixty-four dollar
question is, are you looking for it, too? If the answer's
"yes," I have a fight on my hands.

MELISSA: And if my answer is "no"?

BETH: Then I'll get busy. The apartment he has now won't do. And the right place is so hard to find. Besides, I want to work out this fellowship business. Who spends all that money and how.

MELISSA: I do have one concern.

BETH: I'm listening.

MELISSA: Do you think Dave will have anything to say about this…predicament? Feelings either way?

BETH: None we need worry about. (A beat) Even before I met you, I was certain that either one of us could take care of him. Now I'm more convinced than ever.

MELISSA: In other words, the matter is entirely up to us.

BETH: I'd say so. I know he finds you a bit more elusive, but that doesn't bother me because I have so many other qualities. And, after all, I'll have *him*. You'll turn into a warm memory. And I won't mind that, either.

MELISSA: And if I take him?

BETH: I'll be the warm memory. At school. In his office. (A beat) On the quad. (A beat) Sorry to give you a time limit. I guess that creates some pressure.

MELISSA: Some.

BETH: But I'm sure you can handle it.

MELISSA: I think so.

BETH: Good! Because I think he's ready to pop the question.

MELISSA: Are you sure you can make him ask?

(BETH *stands opposite* MELISSA *and smiles. Pause*)

BETH: And there you have it. If you want him, okay. We can deal with that. But if not, I'd like to know. Before that week at the beach house.

Victor L Cahn

45

MELISSA: I appreciate the warning.

BETH: You're welcome. I hope you don't mind my coming today, but I just had to meet the competition! Now I'm ready to carry on!

MELISSA: It's certainly been...fascinating.

BETH: Same here! *(She removes the shirt.)* Well, I think that covers it. Could I ask one last favor?

MELISSA: I think you've tried on enough clothes—

BETH: No, no—

MELISSA: And I do have to press on.

BETH: I only wanted a little more Pepsi. To fortify myself for the heat!

(A beat)

MELISSA: Of course. *(She goes for the drink.)* Sorry I jumped at you.

BETH: Don't even think about it!

(BETH lays down the shirt and stretches out on the sofa. MELISSA brings her a drink. BETH sips.)

BETH: Thanks *so* much!

(End of Scene 2)

Scene 3

(The following Friday, early afternoon)

(MELISSA, barefoot, sits on the sofa. She alternately eats peanuts and checks her watch.)

(DAVE bursts in.)

DAVE: Hi! I am really sorry!

MELISSA: You made it.

DAVE: Finally! And how are you?

(MELISSA *stands and moves to dump the peanut shells.*
DAVE *tries to kiss her, but misses. He sits on the sofa and*
exhales deeply.)

MELISSA: Everything all right?

DAVE: Now it is. But I am exhausted!

MELISSA: You're also two hours late.

DAVE: I called from the bridge!

MELISSA: I know.

DAVE: And I told you! Traffic was bumper to bumper.
There must've been an accident.

MELISSA: That's what you said.

DAVE: Then my regular garage was full, so I had
to park seven blocks away and walk here. So I am
knocked out! But I made it. *(He breathes deeply.)* And
how are you?

MELISSA: Fine.

DAVE: Good, good.

(A beat)

MELISSA: You seem jumpy.

DAVE: Just trying to catch my breath. *(He stands and*
walks aimlessly.)

MELISSA: I had a nice dinner last night. Alone.

DAVE: And, again, I apologize. But I did call.

MELISSA: That's true.

DAVE: I had to work late, so I called.

MELISSA: I know.

DAVE: Always considerate. That's me. And here I am.

MELISSA: What was the problem last night?

DAVE: I had stuff to take care of.

MELISSA: And did you?

DAVE: What?

MELISSA: Take care of your stuff.

DAVE: Absolutely. Everything and everyone are now in place. *(He looks at his watch.)*

MELISSA: Everyone?

DAVE: My assistant helped. I've mentioned her. Beth.

MELISSA: A couple of times.

DAVE: Wow! That air conditioning feels good. Power was down all over campus this morning. Maybe it was a brownout or something. Anyway, we were really sweatin'.

MELISSA: We?

DAVE: Beth and I. And we had to scramble. Upstairs, downstairs, in and out. I was dripping.

MELISSA: I thought you finished last night.

DAVE: Basically we did, but there were a couple of leftover projects. That's why I got a late start coming here.

MELISSA: You could've opened a window.

DAVE: In the car?

MELISSA: In your office.

DAVE: I thought about that, but Beth said I'd let out whatever cool air we had.

MELISSA: She was probably right.

DAVE: And she was even hotter than I was. *(He looks at his watch.)* All we could do to keep our clothes on! *(He laughs lightly.)*

MELISSA: That hot.

DAVE: Beth said that what we really needed was a Jacuzzi. Right in my office. I told her to put it on next year's budget. *(He laughs)*

MELISSA: Very funny.

DAVE: You had to be there. Anyway, we finished in style.

MELISSA: Too bad for her.

DAVE: Why?

MELISSA: Doesn't she have to stay until later?

DAVE: Normally, but I let her go early. I mean, we were both bushed.

MELISSA: She must have been grateful.

DAVE: I think so. *(A beat)* Y'know, I could use something to drink. How about you?

MELISSA: Sure.

DAVE: Any Diet Pepsi left?

(DAVE goes to the refrigerator. MELISSA sits on the sofa.)

MELISSA: I thought you preferred regular.

DAVE: I used to, but Beth warned me about the sugar. *(He brings out a can that he opens.)* By the way, you're almost out of Pepsi. *(He walks and surreptitiously checks his watch.)*

MELISSA: Something wrong?

DAVE: No. You?

MELISSA: No. But why do you keep checking your watch?

DAVE: I'm not checking it.

MELISSA: Yes, you are.

(DAVE drinks deeply.)

DAVE: Ah! Love that fizz! *(He sips)*

MELISSA: Well?

DAVE: What?

MELISSA: Do you have to be somewhere?

DAVE: No!

MELISSA: But...?

DAVE: No "buts". *(He drinks.)* No "buts". *(A beat)* However...

MELISSA: A "however" is no better than a "but".

DAVE: Well...on the other hand...nevertheless... *(He laughs lightly.)* Synonyms for "but".

MELISSA: You were saying?

DAVE: Right. Uhhh...we may have a little...problem about tonight.

MELISSA: What kind of problem?

DAVE: I think I have to head back to school.

MELISSA: You *think* you have to head back? Or do you actually have to?

DAVE: I think I have to.

MELISSA: Then why show up at all?

DAVE: I figured we'd grab a bite. Anyway, I'm sure you have your own plans.

MELISSA: I don't.

DAVE: You usually do.

MELISSA: Tonight I don't.

DAVE: Oh.

MELISSA: In fact, I set aside this entire weekend for you.

DAVE: Really?

MELISSA: Really.

DAVE: And I can't stay. Too bad.

MELISSA: May I ask why?

DAVE: I have to get back.

MELISSA: Well, that clears that up.

DAVE: You know. Plenty to do.

MELISSA: Let's see. It's Friday afternoon. The end of July. Most people wouldn't think of this as prime academic season.

DAVE: Oh, you'd be surprised. Things are always happening. Summer classes. Special programs.

MELISSA: A regular beehive.

DAVE: That's the word.

MELISSA: But you told me you were going to stay here for the weekend.

DAVE: I thought I would.

MELISSA: So I cancelled two appointments.

DAVE: Now you can make them again.

MELISSA: No, I can't.

DAVE: You can't?

MELISSA: No.

DAVE: Oh. Well, maybe you can call somebody else. With your contacts—

MELISSA: You're avoiding the issue.

DAVE: No, I'm not! Look, you've ducked out on me before!

MELISSA: Is this your revenge?

DAVE: No! *(He begins to pace.)*

MELISSA: Well?

DAVE: Now wait a minute! Isn't this discussion becoming a bit intense?

MELISSA: I don't think so.

DAVE: Let's not lose control, all right? Let's keep calm!

MELISSA: Do I sound intense?

DAVE: There's clearly a note of panic in the air, and I don't think it's helping at all! So let's not panic, okay? Let's stay relaxed.

MELISSA: All right.

DAVE: Good! No matter what happens, and no matter what anyone says, let's keep calm! *(He opens the closet door and takes out his suitcase.)*

MELISSA: What are you doing?

DAVE: Nothing. *(He lays the suitcase open on the table, then goes to the dresser and opens a drawer.)*

MELISSA: Now what?

DAVE: I told you! Nothing! *(He takes out some clothes and puts them in the suitcase.)*

MELISSA: Sure looks like something. In fact, it looks like packing.

DAVE: Just a couple of things that need to be cleaned.

(He takes out some shirts and puts them in the

suitcase)

MELISSA: Weren't those just cleaned?

DAVE: I don't think so. And I'm the one who wears them. And I'm very particular about my clothes.

MELISSA: I never knew that.

DAVE: Well, I am. *(He packs some more clothes.)* Aren't you particular about your clothes?

MELISSA: I suppose so—

DAVE: And do I ever complain about your judgment? No. Because it's a matter of perspective. The person wearing the clothes has a different sense of cleanliness from the person watching the first person wearing the clothes in question. *(He has filled the suitcase.)* Besides, it's time for a change.

MELISSA: A change of what?

(Short pause)

DAVE: All right. Let's get this out in the open. I have to see someone at school. I said I'd be there. And it would very awkward to back out now.

MELISSA: You said you'd stay with me. Isn't it awkward to back out of that?

DAVE: It certainly is.

MELISSA: But this person at school comes ahead of me.

DAVE: I wouldn't put it that way.

MELISSA: How would you put it?

DAVE: I'm talking about a professional commitment. With Beth.

MELISSA: After all the work you finished yesterday, what's left?

DAVE: A lot. We have to go over materials for the fall. Book and film orders. We have to reserve readings in the library. All these things take time. And time is tight.

MELISSA: The semester doesn't start for six weeks.

DAVE: Five and a half.

MELISSA: But you said you caught up this morning.

DAVE: Just the first stage.

(MELISSA peers inside the drawer.)

MELISSA: You're not leaving much.

DAVE: I want a fresh start. *(He closes the suitcase.)*

MELISSA: What about lunch?

DAVE: Maybe we'd better skip it.

MELISSA: You're really in a rush.

DAVE: 'Fraid so. *(A beat)* You see, it's not just the work.

MELISSA: No?

DAVE: It's Beth, too. She made a special appeal for us to be together this weekend.

MELISSA: Didn't you tell her that you were planning to be with me?

DAVE: I did. And she knows all about us. She also knows that I'm a one-woman man. But I felt sorry for her. I hope you understand. *(He picks up the suitcase.)*

MELISSA: Before you go…

DAVE: Yes?

(A beat)

MELISSA: Could we sit for a minute?

DAVE: I'm in a rush.

MELISSA: I know, but this is important. And it won't take long. I promise.

DAVE: Sure it can't wait?

MELISSA: Positive. Don't you have even a little while?

(DAVE shrugs and puts down the suitcase. MELISSA gestures that he should sit on the sofa.)

MELISSA: Over here.

(DAVE sits.)

MELISSA: I need to talk something over with you.

DAVE: 'kay. What's up?

MELISSA: Well, I haven't mentioned it, but I've been working on a screenplay.

DAVE: Really! Aren't you bold?

MELISSA: I'm trying.

DAVE: And how's it going?

MELISSA: Pretty well. But I've reached a crucial stage, and I need your help.

DAVE: Anything I can do.

MELISSA: Thanks. Now here's the plot. It's about this guy, an academic. His name is Don. And he's in love with this girl, a writer. Her name is Michelle.

DAVE: Sounds familiar.

MELISSA: Thought it might. Now, they love each other, but even though he wants to marry her, she isn't ready to marry him.

DAVE: Sounds more familiar all the time.

MELISSA: But here's the complication. One day Michelle gets a visit from Don's assistant.

DAVE: You mean a girl like Beth?

MELISSA: Could be.

DAVE: I get it. This is the imaginary part, right?

(A beat)

MELISSA: Right.

DAVE: And what's her name?

MELISSA: I call her…"Babs".

DAVE: Babs. I like it!

MELISSA: Good. Now, the way I see it, when Babs drops by Michelle's apartment, the two begin to talk about Don.

DAVE: And what do they say?

MELISSA: Well, before long Babs makes it very clear that she wants Don for herself. She also makes it clear that Michelle is in her way.

DAVE: Sounds tense.

MELISSA: Meanwhile Michelle realizes that Babs is an extremely determined young woman.

DAVE: How can she be sure?

MELISSA: Trust me. She's sure. Babs also claims that she is very close to getting Don to marry her.

DAVE: And is she convincing?

MELISSA: She claims she's got Don wrapped around her little finger.

DAVE: Wow.

MELISSA: Wow, indeed. But Michelle still has a lot of questions. And here's where everything becomes messy.

DAVE: And dramatically compelling, right?

MELISSA: I hope so.

DAVE: Go on.

MELISSA: Well, first, does Don know that Babs has visited? Or is he completely in the dark?

DAVE: What do you think?

MELISSA: I don't know. I mean, Babs claims she's operating on her own.

DAVE: But why would she come at all?

MELISSA: What do you think?

DAVE: Maybe she's trying to frighten Michelle off. Girls do that, don't they?

MELISSA: It's been known to happen.

DAVE: Is that what Michelle thinks?

MELISSA: She's not sure.

DAVE: And I know why.

MELISSA: Why?

DAVE: Because there's another possibility.

MELISSA: Which is …?

DAVE: That Don is so desperate to get Michelle to marry him that he tells Babs to pretend to be interested in him just to make Michelle jealous.

MELISSA: Would a man do that?

DAVE: He might. And what a great twist.

MELISSA: But hold on. If Babs loves Don, would she be willing to risk making Michelle so jealous that the scheme backfires and Michelle runs to Don?

DAVE: Maybe she's willing to take that chance. On the other hand, maybe Don doesn't know that Babs is in love with him, so he figures she'll simply follow orders.

MELISSA: In other words, he may be too blind to realize that Babs has her own agenda.

DAVE: Right. So she's telling Don one thing…

MELISSA: …and going another way with Michelle.

DAVE: Exactly.

MELISSA: Told you it was complicated.

DAVE: And you were right. But before we can resolve any of these issues, we have to know what kind of a guy Don is. Is he capable of being so manipulative?

MELISSA: Hard to say. After all, Michelle figures he's pretty straightforward. Bright, warm, funny, and totally without guile.

DAVE: That's probably why she loves him.

MELISSA: But if in fact he sent Babs…

DAVE: He may be a lot trickier than she thinks. I mean, that's a pretty diabolical maneuver.

MELISSA: Right. So I have to decide whether Don could be such a mastermind.

DAVE: And what do you think?

MELISSA: What do *you* think?

DAVE: I don't know. But let's go with that idea. Let's say that Michelle thinks that Don sent Babs to make her jealous.

MELISSA: Okay.

DAVE: Which leads to another big question: does the possibility that Don sent Babs make him more or less attractive to Michelle?

MELISSA: Could be either one.

DAVE: Could be.

MELISSA: Or it could be both.

DAVE: Could be.

MELISSA: But before I decide…

DAVE: Yes?

MELISSA: Let's consider one more point of confusion. Suppose Don did tell Babs to make Michelle jealous, but he's not aware of how Babs mocks him.

DAVE: Or…maybe Don told Babs to act that way in order to discourage Michelle by making him sound so weak.

MELISSA: Or maybe Babs simply has her own strategy.

DAVE: Or maybe Babs's entire performance is part of Don's strategy.

MELISSA: Do you see how involved it is? Michelle has no way of knowing the truth. In the meantime Don is threatening to pack and leave, and Michelle has to decide what to do. And here's where I'm stuck.

DAVE: I can see why. *(A beat)* I have an idea.

MELISSA: Yes?

DAVE: Let's improvise some dialogue. Right from this point. I'll play Don. You play Michelle.

MELISSA: You mean act out a scene?

DAVE: And see where we end up. Might solve the whole problem.

MELISSA: Sounds reasonable.

(DAVE *motions to* MELISSA.)

MELISSA: You want me to start?

DAVE: Why not?

MELISSA: Okay. Well...*Don*...here's one alternative. You can pack your clothes and head out to do whatever you want to do with your assistant.

DAVE: Or...

MELISSA: Or you can leave your clothes and continue to stay here a few days each week with me. That about covers it.

DAVE: Okay. Well, then...*Michelle*...how would you feel if you knew that while I stayed a few days each week with you, I...perhaps...spent the other few days with Babs? And maybe some other people.

MELISSA: Only if it would bother you that while you were staying a few days each week with Babs as well as other people, I was also staying with other people.

DAVE: That would bother me.

MELISSA: And the same thing on your part would bother me.

DAVE: Then we've cut down on the possibilities.

(A beat. At the moment DAVE *and* MELISSA *are far apart, but slowly begin to draw together.)*

MELISSA: There is, however, at least one more possibility.

DAVE: Probably more than one.

MELISSA: But I'm thinking this way. You might leave all your other partners out of the picture.

DAVE: All of them?

MELISSA: Particularly Babs.

DAVE: Completely out of the picture.

MELISSA: In every way. Professionally and personally.

DAVE: I could do that.

MELISSA: Happy to hear it.

DAVE: But it might not solve the whole problem. Because I'd want you to leave a few fellows out of the picture as well.

MELISSA: Go on.

DAVE: In fact, you'd have to leave *all* the others fellows out of the picture.

MELISSA: Every single one?

DAVE: Single, married. Every one.

MELISSA: That would leave me with just you.

DAVE: And me with just you.

MELISSA: Would that be…satisfactory?

DAVE: For me or for you?

MELISSA: Both of us, I hope.

DAVE: I agree. In fact, I think we'd be getting close to a resolution.

MELISSA: What's missing?

DAVE: According to this agreement, I'm alone at school three or four nights a week.

MELISSA: While I'm all by myself. Not good.

DAVE: No. But I do have a suggestion.

MELISSA: I like it already.

DAVE: You haven't heard it.

MELISSA: I think I know what's coming.

DAVE: Then I'll say it. We could live together seven nights a week.

MELISSA: What do you know? I was right.

DAVE: Were you? I'm glad we're seeing things the same way. Then again...

MELISSA: Yes?

DAVE: If we follow this course of action, we might find ourselves taking certain celebrated legal steps.

MELISSA: You mean...

DAVE: License, minister...

MELISSA: Guests, party...

DAVE: What we once described as "the works".

MELISSA: But then quite a few details would have to be settled.

DAVE: A familiar litany of challenges. But I don't think any would be insurmountable.

MELISSA: In that case, we're probably close to a decision.

DAVE: Of course, all this activity will complicate our lives beyond anything we can imagine.

MELISSA: Certainly. But we'll just have to...discuss everything.

DAVE: Sounds reasonable. *(A bet)* I think I'm ready to make a decison. How about you?

MELISSA: First let's clear up one point. Are you still acting with Michelle?

DAVE: Actually, I'm talking to Melissa.

MELISSA: Which means I'm talking to Dave.

DAVE: Present.

(A beat)

MELISSA: You really think we can handle all the problems?

DAVE: If we do it together.

MELISSA: That would mean you're my guy.

DAVE: I would be indeed.

MELISSA: And all those other guys...

DAVE: No longer matter.

MELISSA: Because I have you.

(A beat)

DAVE: I'm your guy.

(DAVE *and* MELISSA *kiss.*)

DAVE: I guess we've solved your screenplay problem.

MELISSA: And a lot more.

(DAVE *and* MELISSA *embrace.*)

DAVE: Hmmm.

MELISSA: What?

DAVE: Just wondering if I should call Beth.

MELISSA: Why bother?

DAVE: To tell her that I'm not showing up today.

MELISSA: Did you say you'd call?

DAVE: Only if I'm coming home.

MELISSA: And since you're not...

DAVE: Then there's no need to call.

MELISSA: Right. But you should call later.

DAVE: Why?

MELISSA: So she can start looking for a new job.

DAVE: You want me to fire her?

MELISSA: You won't have to. Just explain our plans, and she'll quit.

DAVE: You sure?

MELISSA: I guarantee it. And if she's as good as you say, she won't have any trouble landing a new position.

DAVE: I don't want to hurt her.

MELISSA: I bet she's stronger than you think.

DAVE: Almost sounds as if you know her. *(A beat. He laughs lightly.)* Funny, isn't it?

MELISSA: What?

DAVE: Talking about Beth seems to have brought us together. Maybe I should have mentioned her earlier.

(A beat)

MELISSA: What do you mean?

DAVE: Nothing. Only that for all this time I've been trying to get you to marry me. And as soon as I mentioned Beth, everything changed.

MELISSA: Coincidence.

DAVE: Probably. *(A beat)* I'm also *very* glad that you two never met.

MELISSA: Why? Is she so attractive?

DAVE: No, no, no, no! Oh, she's cute. But no way she's in your league.

MELISSA: You're sweet. (*Á la* BETH) *Thanks SO much!*

(DAVE *straightens and stares at* MELISSA)

MELISSA: Something wrong?

DAVE: You sounded like…

MELISSA: Who?

DAVE: Never mind.

(*A beat*)

MELISSA: One more thing. Has there ever been anybody else but me?

DAVE: I told you. Nobody.

MELISSA: But how can I be sure?

DAVE: Let's put it this way. With all the guys you've known, has there ever been anybody else but me?

(*A beat*)

MELISSA: No.

DAVE: And I believe you. But deep down…way, way deep down, how can I know for sure?

MELISSA: I told you: you have to trust me.

DAVE: And that's just what *you* have to do: trust me.

MELISSA: You mean we have to believe in each other.

DAVE: That's it.

MELISSA: Sounds perfect.

DAVE: Almost perfect.

MELISSA: What's wrong?

DAVE: It'll be perfect when you finish your article, when your editor accepts it, and when he tells you that it's the best work you've ever done. Because it is. *Then* everything will be perfect.

MELISSA: Thank you.

DAVE: You're welcome.

(DAVE *and* MELISSA *smile at each other.)*

MELISSA: I'll get dressed, and we can go out.

DAVE: Great.

(MELISSA *goes into the bedroom.* DAVE *pours a drink, and sips, leans back, then raises the glass as if making a toast.)*

DAVE: *(Á la* BETH*)* Thanks *so-o-o* much!

(As HE smiles, MELISSA *pokes her head out)*

MELISSA: Did you say something?

DAVE: No.

(MELISSA *withdraws. As* DAVE *smiles broadly, she peers out quizzically.)*

(Curtain)

END OF PLAY

www.ingramcontent.com/pod-product-compliance
Lightning Source LLC
Chambersburg PA
CBHW070026110426
42741CB00034B/2607